# FULLY GORGEOUS

## Fantastic Outfits from History

### *Let's Travel Back in Time!*

History is all about the past. Some people think the past is dead and buried. It happened so long ago. Who cares now? Right? Wrong! The past is all around us. We can read about it in books. We can see it in old pictures. We can visit old places and imagine what they were like many, many years ago. It's like travelling back in time!

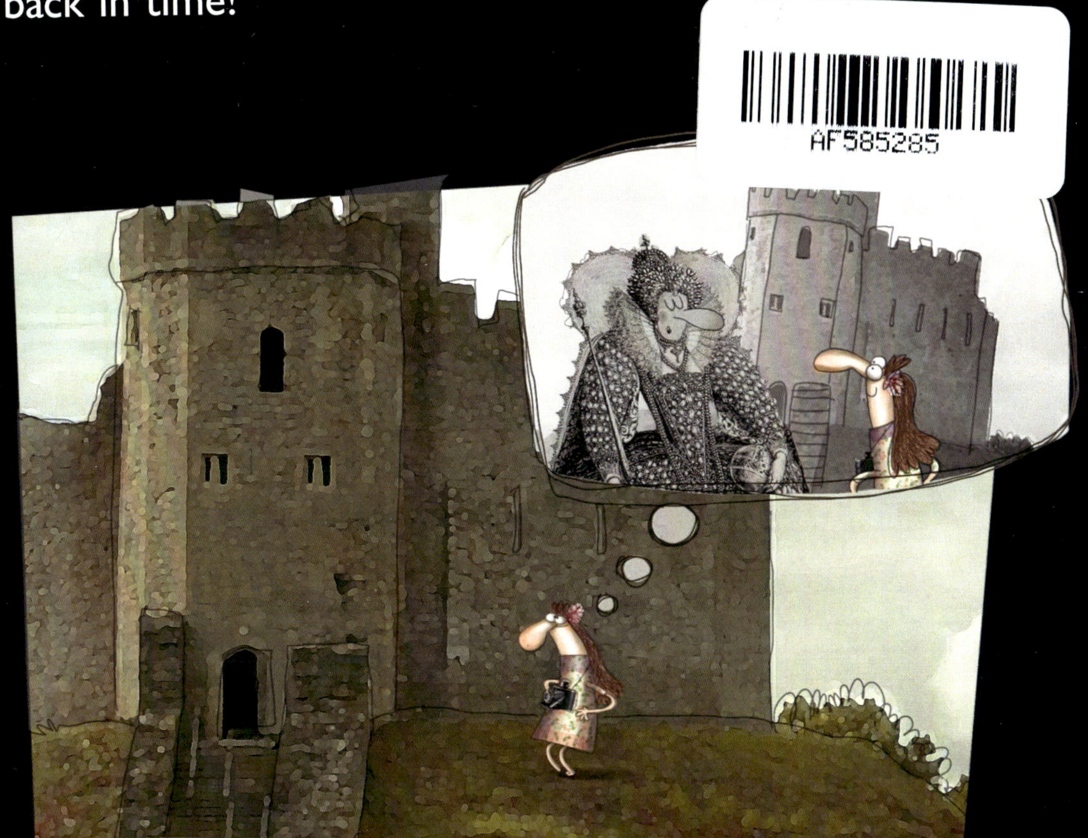

# Contents

Have you ever wondered what wacky outfits people wore in the past? Well, now's your chance to find out! Imagine a time before jeans and T-shirts. A time before zips and buttons. How did people cope? What did people wear? And most importantly, did they look fully gorgeous?

It takes money to look this good!

## Chapter 1
# *Dress to Impress*

A lot of people today like to look fully gorgeous. So did people in the past. You'll soon see what outfits they wore. But first, here are some facts that might surprise you about the history of fashion.

### *Who Cares About Fashion?*

You may think that fashion is just for girls. But in the past, both men and women wanted to look gorgeous. They went out of their way to do this and wore some truly eye-popping outfits.

## *Expensive Fashions*

Not all men and women could wear gorgeous clothes like the ones in this book. Only rich people could really afford to buy them. They paid a **tailor** or a **dressmaker** to make their clothes by hand.

Most people only owned a few clothes. Usually they had to make their clothes themselves. They used rough, cheap **fabrics** and had to wear them until they fell apart.

## *Dressing Up Like Mum and Dad*

In the past, it wasn't easy to tell a very young boy from a very young girl. Why not? Because they wore clothes that looked exactly the same.

Then, as they got older, children wore smaller versions of grown-ups' clothes. It was really easy to see who came from a rich family and who didn't. Poorer children had rough, "homemade" clothes just like their parents. Rich children had fine clothes just like *their* parents, too.

## *Different Times in History*

Before we start looking at old fashions, let's get a few things clear.

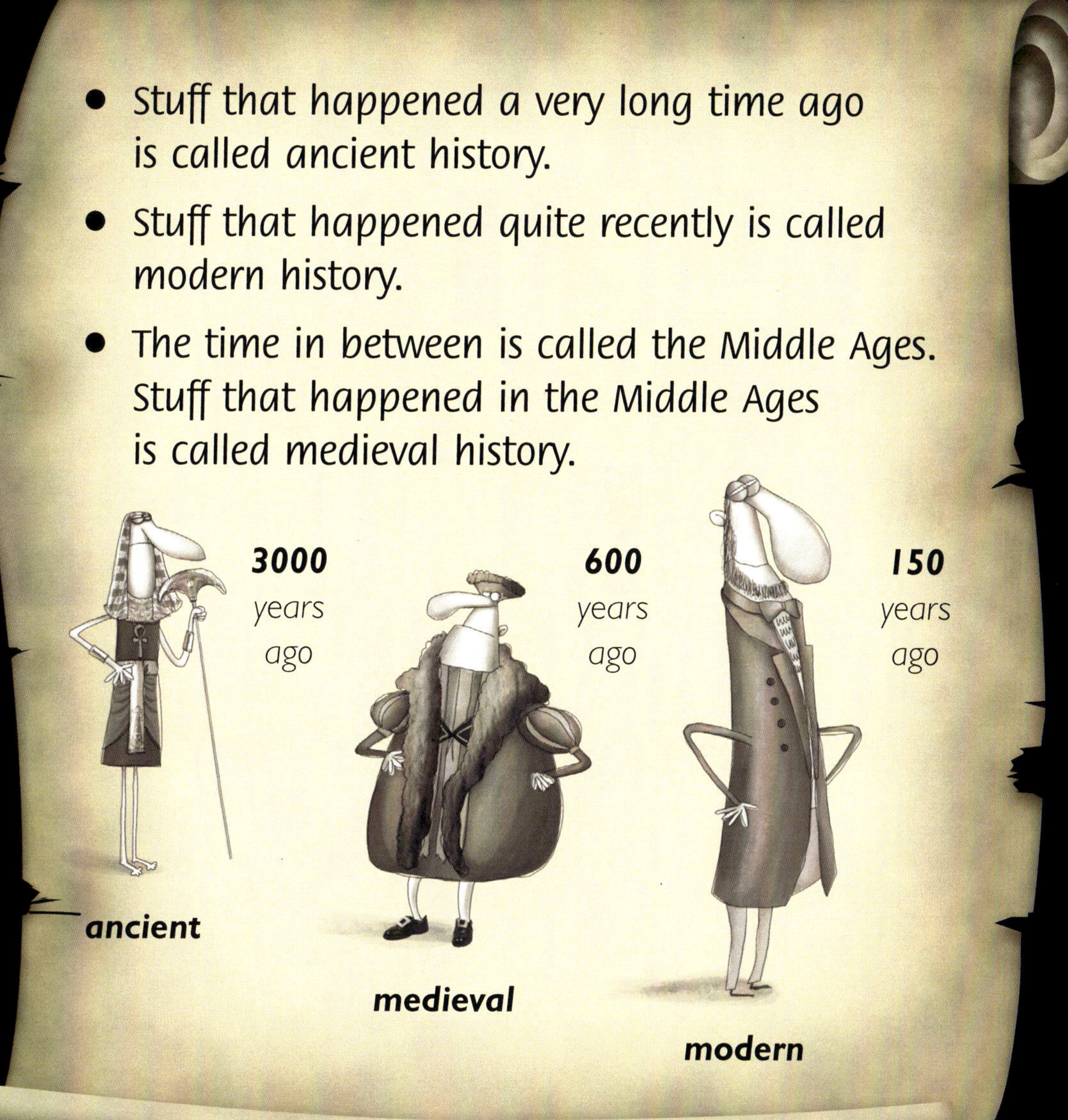


Got all that? Great! Fasten your seatbelts. Let's travel back to ancient history first.

Let's chill!

## Chapter 2
## ***Extremely Cool Egyptians***

***Time:*** *3000–4000 years ago*
***Place:*** *Ancient Egypt in North Africa*

Egyptian people didn't just want to look cool – they wanted to feel cool, too! Egypt was very, very hot, so the Egyptians came up with some wacky ways to keep themselves chilled…

## *Who Is Who?*

Rich Egyptian men liked to look as good as their wives. In fact, they often looked quite similar!

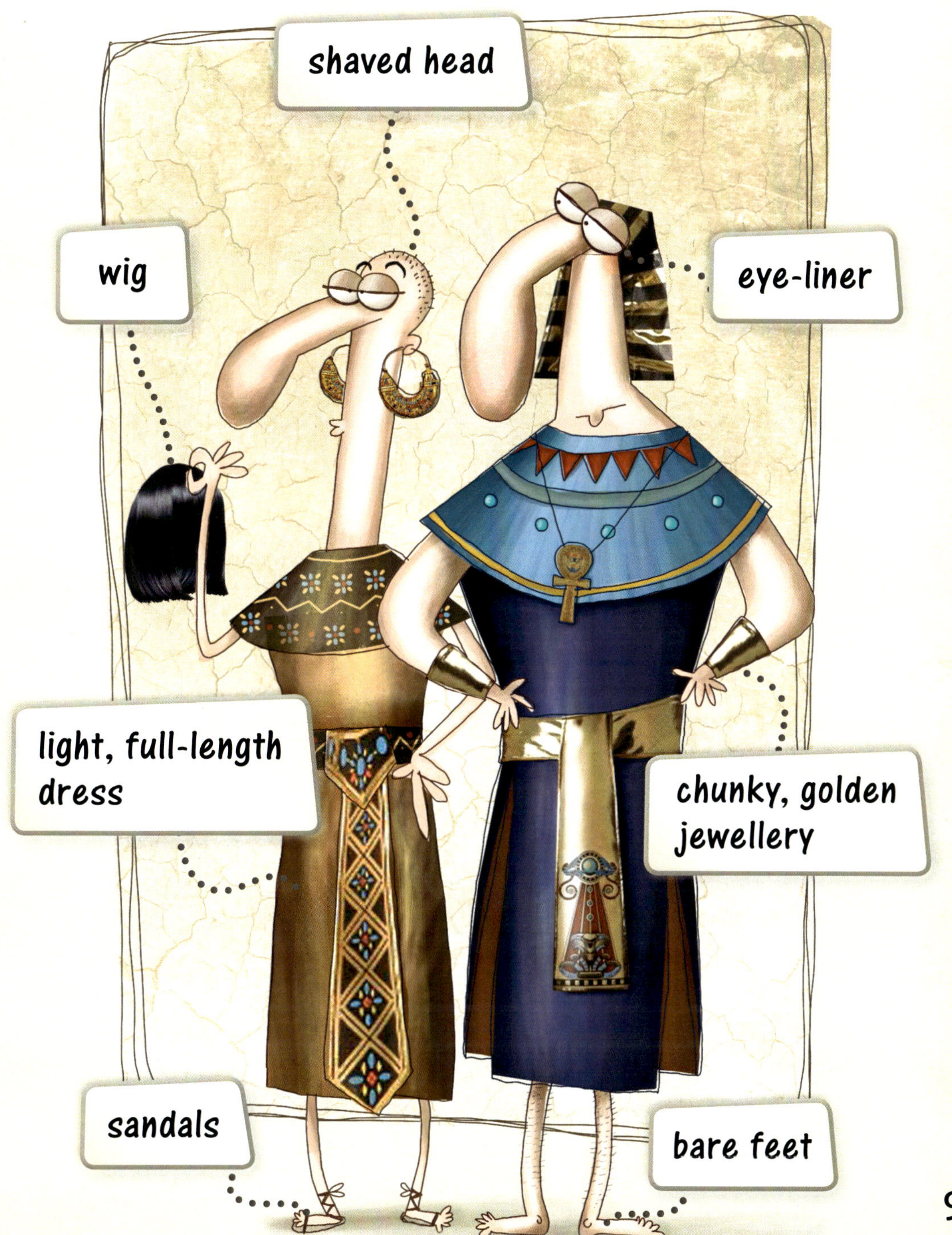

This Egyptian man and his wife were fully fashionable about 3350 years ago.

### *Clothes Fit for a King*

Fashionable Egyptians wore clothes made of cotton or linen. These fabrics kept them cool. Egypt's kings, called pharaohs, wore clothes made with gold thread. Poorer people had to make do with clothes made out of dried **reeds**!

## *Cool Hair*

Fashionable Egyptians also wore wigs, which made their heads quite hot. So, how could they look cool *and* keep a cool head?

Today, fashions seem to change every week. In ancient times, new styles came along much less often. Now, let's jump ahead to see how fully gorgeous the ancient Greeks and Romans were...

I want more, more, more!

Chapter 3

# Greeks and Romans – All Wrapped Up

**Time:** *2000–3000 years ago*

**Place:** *Ancient Greece and Rome in Southern Europe*

The ancient Greeks and Romans wore heavier clothes than the Egyptians. They loved to wrap themselves up in big, loose **garments**. Both men and women tried very hard to look fully gorgeous!

Look at the gorgeous Greek woman below getting ready to go out. Oh, hang on, it's not a woman, it's a man. Rich Greek men spent lots and LOTS of time getting ready to go out.

Rich Greek women didn't go out much at all. They were supposed to stay at home, to run the house and bring up children. But that didn't stop rich women dressing up, even if no one got to see how gorgeous they looked!

## *Long Chitons and Tricky Togas*

Greek men and women draped themselves in chitons (say: *ky-tons*). A chiton was made from a lot of material. You could:

- wear it loose and just let it hang
- use a belt to pull it in at the waist
- use the folds to make sleeves
- use a fold to make a hood!

In ancient Rome, a little later than in Greece, rich women wore beautiful long robes and colourful shawls. The men wore togas (say: *toe-gers*). Togas were like big, oval-shaped blankets and were tricky to put on.

## PUT ON YOUR TOGA IN 4 EASY STEPS

1. Put one end over your left shoulder.

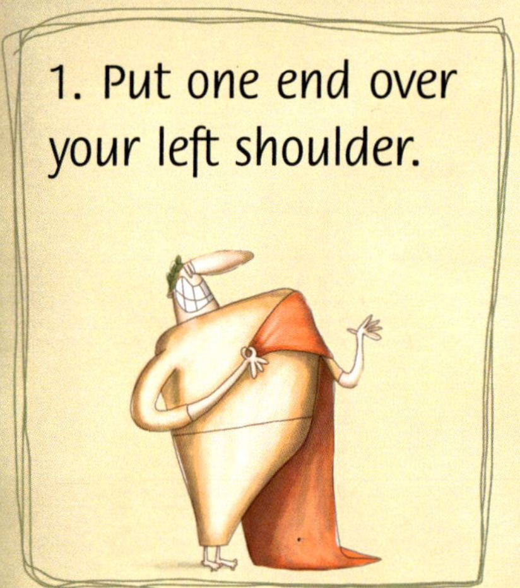

2. Bring the other end under your right arm.

3. Put the right end over your left shoulder, too.

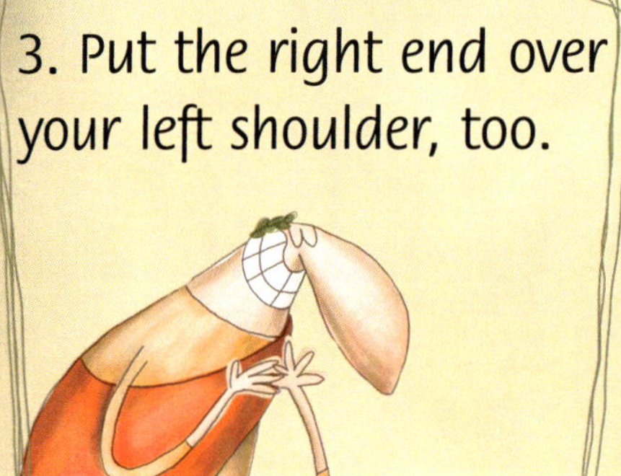

4. Tuck the middle into the belt of your tunic.

**Now you look *gorgeous* and are ready to go out!**

## *Toga Rules*

There were strict rules about the colours togas could be. For example, important men had a purple border on their togas. The size of your toga also showed how important you were. Some togas were massive – 5.5 metres long and 3.5 metres wide!

The ancient Greeks and Romans loved loose clothes. But 1000 years later, the baggy look was totally over...

Is my hat big enough?

## Chapter 4
# *Tight Fits from France*

***Time:*** *The Middle Ages, about 600 years ago*
***Place:*** *France and Western Europe*

By the 1400s, Europe's richest people had gone fashion crazy! New styles spread from country to country and fashion was all about showing off!

## Medieval Fashion Tips

- Don't hide yourself in baggy clothes.
- Show your slender arms, girls!
- Show your shapely legs, guys!
- Think of the fabrics you can wear – velvets, silks and furs in all the colours of the rainbow!
- Greeks and Romans are ancient history.
- Move with the times – GET MEDIEVAL!

## *Tight Fits*

Rich medieval women loved showing off their figures. They wore dresses with narrow waists and tight sleeves. They wore thick velvet gowns to keep out the winter chill.

Men wore decorated tunics called doublets (say: *dub-lets*). On their legs they wore tight leggings called hose. There wasn't any room for pockets, so they had purses on their belts instead.

### *Extraordinary Hats and Shoes*

But not *all* the clothes in medieval times were figure-hugging. When it came to heads and feet, BIG was BEAUTIFUL!

This old painting shows a medieval couple getting married. They clearly think they look fully gorgeous, don't they?

Look at the woman's huge hat. These hats could be as much as 1.2 metres high. That's almost as tall as the woman herself!

Look at the man's shoes. Men in medieval Europe loved long, pointy shoes. The longer the shoes, the more fashionable the man!

In England, a law said rich people could wear shoes up to 61 centimetres long! But ordinary people's shoes could not be longer than 15 centimetres.

Not everyone thought that big was better. In fact, one **Parisian bishop** thought that using so much fabric to make one dress was very wasteful indeed.

Other medieval people also thought fashion had become *too* crazy. But as time went on, fashion didn't become more sensible. In fact, it went totally over the top...

Does my neck look fat in this?

Chapter 5

# Over-the-Top Tudors

**Time:** *The Tudor period, 400–500 years ago*
**Place:** *England and Europe*

Rich Tudor people dressed to make a BIG impression. The bigger the clothes, the better. But that meant they wore some very strange outfits.

Take a look at this. It's made from hoops of **whalebone** sewn into fabric. What do you think it is?

It is called a farthingale. Tudor women wore them under their dresses. Why? To make their skirts big and wide!

### ***Big Is Best***

It wasn't just the women who thought that big was beautiful. A new fashion from Spain really excited Tudor men. It was called a ruff and it was a fancy collar. It was so big that wires were used to hold it up!

## Tudor Troubles

### Tell Aunty Anne all your woes.

**Hungry Harry:** I love wearing Spanish ruffs. But my ruff is so wide I'm finding it hard to get food into my mouth. I'm afraid I'll starve to death! What can I do?

**Aunty Anne:** My dear man, all you need is a long-handled spoon!

Rich, important Tudor people paid a lot of money for stiff, uncomfortable clothes – but somehow they still managed to dance...

You can also see that they wore big, padded sleeves. Sometimes they had slashes in their clothes, too. This was to show off the layers of clothing underneath.

Big really was best in Tudor times. But how did the rich people know this was in fashion? There weren't any fashion magazines back then.

## *Fashionable Dolls*

Tudor women had dolls to keep on top of the latest fashions. Every detail of the doll's dress was correct. The dressmaker just copied what the doll was wearing.

Make me a dress in the latest French style.

Certainly, madam. What does that look like?

The Tudors knew how to impress with their big fashions. But did clothes just keep getting bigger? Did men keep looking as flashy as women?

## Chapter 6
# *Sensible Victorians*

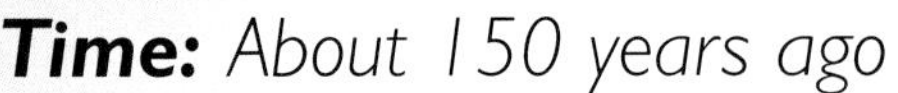


***Time:*** *About 150 years ago*

***Place:*** *Europe, Britain, the USA and Australia*

In the mid-1800s, fashions finally became more sensible. There were also big changes in how clothes were made and bought.

The queen who ruled Britain at the time was called Victoria. We now call the people who lived then "Victorians". Rich Victorian men and women weren't as flashy as the Tudors. They still wanted to look fully gorgeous, but in less crazy ways.

Women still liked to show off their tiny waists. They wore very tight, stiff garments called corsets under their clothes, to make their waists really small. Their real waists weren't quite as small as they appeared!

Men wore smart, sensible coats. They also wore trousers. When bicycles were invented, women wore trousers called bloomers. They couldn't ride their bikes in huge dresses!

## *More Change in the Fashion World*

Not all Victorian outfits were made by hand. Special machines were used to make different types of fabrics. Then, sewing machines were invented. Making clothes had never been so quick! But an even bigger change was on the way...

### *Ready-Made Clothes*

Around 1860, the first **fashion houses** opened. These were places where rich people could buy new outfits. Top **designers** created the clothes so they cost a lot!

7 February 1861

My dear,

Have you heard of the latest thing? You no longer need to tell your dressmaker what clothes to make you. Now you go to a fashion house and simply pick a dress that has already been made! The Queen shops at these places, too!

Best wishes,
Lady Dale

But you didn't need a queen's riches to buy stylish clothes. Less wealthy Victorian men and women shopped at **department stores**. They could buy cheaper copies of what the rich people were wearing!

For the first time ever, people could also buy outfits made just for children. These outfits were still based on what the adults wore. Sailor suits for little boys were very popular.

By the early 1900s, it was becoming easier and cheaper for many people to buy the latest fashions. You didn't have to be mega rich to be fully gorgeous any more!

# Chapter 7
## *Well, Are You Impressed?*

Now you've seen just a few of the ways people used to dress to impress. Would *you* like to wear one of these eye-popping outfits?

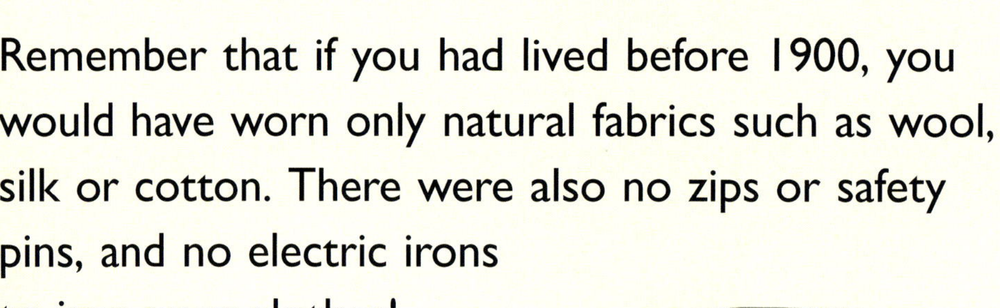

Remember that if you had lived before 1900, you would have worn only natural fabrics such as wool, silk or cotton. There were also no zips or safety pins, and no electric irons to iron your clothes!

Last of all, remember: only a tiny number of men, women and children ever really got to look fully gorgeous – they were the rich. Most people's clothes were old, smelly and uncomfortable – not much fun at all!

So, the modern clothes you are wearing are probably a lot more comfortable! But you could still wear a fully gorgeous outfit from the past to your next fancy dress party!

## *Timeline*

Here are some of the fully gorgeous fashions we have looked at.

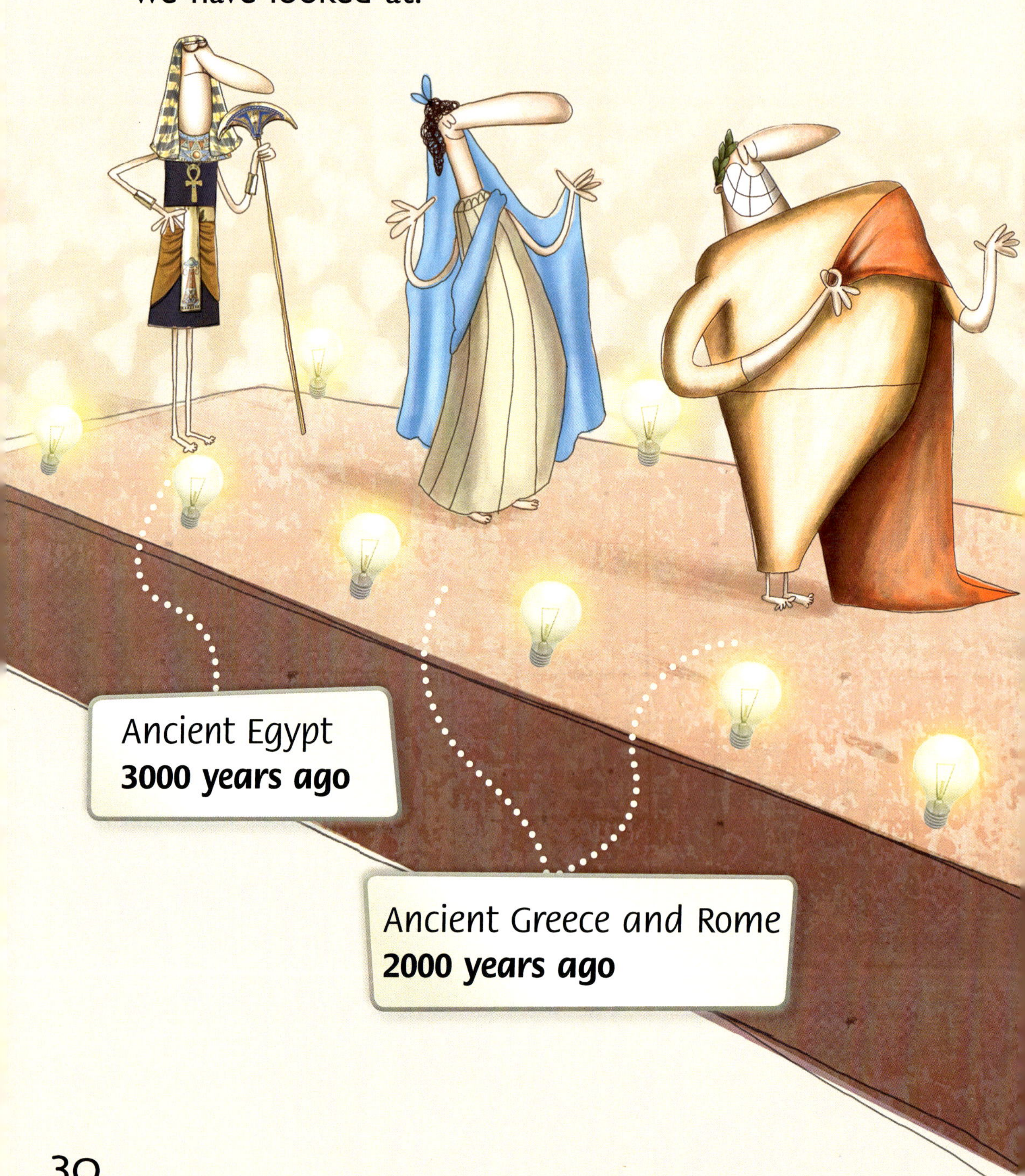

Medieval Times
600 years ago
Tudor Times
450 years ago
Victorian Times
150 years ago

# Glossary

**bishop:** important person in the Christian Church

**department stores:** large shops with separate areas, each selling a certain type of thing

**designers:** people who plan how clothes should look

**dressmaker:** someone who makes clothes for women

**fabrics:** materials used to make clothes

**fashion houses:** businesses that design, make and sell clothes

**garments:** items of clothing

**Parisian:** from or of Paris, France

**reeds:** tall grasses that grow in marshy places

**tailor:** someone who makes clothes, especially for men

**whalebone:** piece of bone from a whale used to make clothes stiff

# Index